D1023484

THE
ANATOMY
OF A
DISCIPLE

SO MANY BELIEVERS. SO FEW DISCIPLES.

A DISCIPLESHIP GUIDE

DR. RICK TAYLOR

Copyright © 2014 by The Well Community Church

To request additional information, book speaking engagements or request bulk purchase
pricing, go to anatomyofadisciple.com.

GUIDELINES FOR
DISCIPLES

- Spend a few minutes asking God to help you understand and process the material each week.

- Have your Bible with you as you work through the material.

- Work all the way through the material each week.

- If you are meeting with someone else or in a group, work through the material before you meet.

- Come prepared to share.

- Be sure to write out verses of Scripture when you are asked. This is an important and proven part of the whole discipleship process.

- If you want to go deeper each week, consider reading *The Anatomy of a Disciple: So Many Believers. So Few Disciples.* by Dr. Rick Taylor as you work through the material. Chapters to read are recommended at the beginning of each week's material.

GUIDELINES FOR
LEADERS

- It would be valuable for you to read and study *The Anatomy of a Disciple: So Many Believers. So Few Disciples.* by Dr. Rick Taylor.

- If you are taking another person or a small group through the material, it would be helpful to emphasize the importance of them reading and following the Guidelines for Disciples.

- Part of the goal of this process is to help prepare those you are leading through this material to be able to lead others when you are finished.

TABLE OF CONTENTS

WEEK 1
ON BECOMING AND BEING A DISCIPLE OF JESUS

When I was seven years old my mom took me to a revival service at her church. The focus of the message was on hell, painting a very vivid picture of what it would be like. The preacher did a good job of scaring the hell out of this one young little fella, because on the way home I started crying and told my parents that I was scared of going to hell, and didn't want to go there, no matter what.

And that set off a chain of events. First my parents didn't know what to do. So they called the pastor of the church and he rushed over to our home late that night. There was a lot of crying and loud ranting they called prayer, all on the part of my mom and the pastor. This scared me almost as much as the evangelist had done earlier.

They put their hands on me and continued very loudly, and with great emotion they declared that I was a Christian and safe from hell.

As horrifying as everything else had been that evening, this was at last a great relief to know that I wasn't going to hell.

In the years ahead, I grew up going to various churches, and I heard a fair share of sermons and messages. And I was safe from hell. Why? Because no Christian goes to hell and I had been declared a Christian

5

by a pastor when I was seven. I had gone to church fairly regularly since then, I was a mostly moral person—at least compared to other people I could compare myself to—and I was born in America, and wasn't a Hindu or Muslim, so I must be a Christian.

It was the weekend before I started college that I went on a church retreat for all the wrong reasons, the main one being there were some girls going on the retreat that I wanted to get to know better.

I wanted to meet girls. But God wanted me to meet Him.

The very first night of the retreat there was a gathering in a pavilion on the grounds of the state park where we were staying. The leaders, Jack and Joel, shared their stories of how they had met Jesus and how He had changed their lives. My first thought was that they must have had the same experience as I did when I was seven.

But they told a different story. They talked about the reality that we all live lives different from God and His way of life. They called that sin. Being a Christian was not about trying to be good, or better than most or having some sort of experience. It was about Jesus and putting your faith in Him.

They went on to explain that the penalty for living life different than God was being separated from Him forever. But God had sent His God-Son, Jesus, to die on the cross and pay the penalty for our sin.

I had believed that Jesus came, died, rose from the dead and went back to heaven. But I had no idea why. Now I was hearing for the first time that it was my sin that put Jesus on the cross. And it was my sin that He paid for when He died.

After expressing a number of questions and concerns to the leaders, I received Jesus' gift of forgiveness and new life through a prayer of faith. Now I was indeed a Christian, and I had an assurance of both forgiveness and a new kind of life like never before.

1. Write out John 3:16 below.

2. What was your life like before you met Jesus in a personal way?

3. When and where did you come to understand that Jesus died and paid the penalty for your sin?

4. How did you personally receive Jesus' gift of forgiveness and new life?

I followed Jesus for many years after I accepted His forgiveness. I was a believer. I was a pastor, living like a Christian. My life was good and my faith was real. And there were moments of living out my faith that were very strong and growing. But the general tenor of my Christian life was increasingly flat and empty. No one but me would have probably ever known.

It was in my car, driving down Interstate 5 from Eugene, Oregon to Oakland, California that changed everything. I was hoping the time in Oakland would be a spiritual uplift for me. Instead, it was the trip in the car with just me and God—and Keith Green:

My eyes are dry, my faith is old,
My heart is hard, my prayers are cold...
Oh what can be done, for an old heart like mine[1]

The words of that old Keith Green song captured my attention. I pushed repeat and listened to those words again. And again. And again, until it was no longer Keith Green's song and it wasn't him singing. It was my song, and I was singing those words with a depth of conviction

1 Keith Green, "My Eyes Are Dry" (Sparrow Records, 1978).

and passion I had not felt for a long time. Tears flooded my eyes and my heart was pounding in my chest.

In those moments alone in the car, I found myself singing a confession to God: "MY eyes are dry and MY faith is old. MY heart is hard and MY prayers are cold. And I cried out, "Oh God, what can be done for an old heart like MINE?"

It was in that long car ride that I came face to face with my living, all-powerful Lord. He had captured my attention. I finished the trip with a conviction that something had to change. I did not know what it would look like, but I began the journey from being merely a follower to becoming a growing disciple of Jesus Christ.

5. How have you seen your life change since becoming a Christian?

6. Have you had times when you felt like you were going through the motions of being a Christian? What were those times like for you?

7. Where are you at right now in your faith-life relationship with Jesus? Are you experiencing abundant life, settling for an adequate life, or something else? Describe it.

8. What do you hope to get out of this study?

WEEK 2
GOD IS REFASHIONING YOU INTO THE IMAGE OF JESUS

RECOMMENDED READING
THE ANATOMY OF A DISCIPLE CHAPTERS 1-2

Discipleship is all about change. God is the orchestrator of this change, and He can and has answered the question, "Change to what?" He has also revealed His strategy for how that change works in your life.

Both as a disciple and a discipler, you need to understand discipleship from God's perspective.

1. Write out Matthew 28:18-20 below.

2. What are some of your observations about these statements of Jesus?

Based on the authority over all things the Father had bestowed on His Son, Jesus gave His followers one last command, more in the form of a commissioning into service. He told them to "make disciples." This is the only imperative (command) in these verses; "go," "baptizing" and "teaching" are all participles that describe how to make disciples.

In the Old and New Testaments, a disciple was one who followed a teacher, with the intent of becoming like them. A disciple follows the teacher to learn from him, observe how he lives and then learn to live like him. That is what Jesus called His disciples to do and what He calls you to do: follow Him for the purpose of becoming more like Him.

3. What are some of the cheap substitutes for being a true disciple (one who follows Jesus for the purpose of becoming like Him) that are easy to fall for?

4. Is your life becoming more like Christ? What is encouraging and discouraging to you in this process?

5. Who are some of the people you aspired to be as you were growing up? What was it about them that you wanted to be true in your life?

6. Write out Genesis 1:26-27 below.

7. The word used in these verses for *image* is often translated "idol." It means a physical, tangible representative of a greater reality (in this case God Himself). What does it mean that you were created in the image of God?

8. What happened to the image of God in mankind in Genesis 3:6-13? (Pay particular attention to indications of shame, guilt, fear and blame shifting.)

9. How does Paul describe this result in mankind in Romans 3:10-18?

10. Write out Ephesians 4:11-13 below.

11. Even though the image of God is marred, what do these verses tell you about God's design for you today regarding the image of God in you?

12. Is it hard for you to believe that you can be conformed to the image of Jesus? If so, why?

13. What has God most impressed upon you personally from this study? Express this in a written prayer to God below.

WEEK 3
GOD IS AT WORK TO CHANGE EVERY AREA OF YOUR LIFE

RECOMMENDED READING
THE ANATOMY OF A DISCIPLE CHAPTERS 3-4

1. What are some of the frustrations you have had with your spiritual growth in the past?

Most Christians have applied the popular idea of behavior modification to Christianity and the church. You try to *look* different and *act* differently, like a Christian. And we often call that the growing Christian life.

But deep inside, in the wellspring out of which real life comes, you are unchanged. You have learned to put on the face of what you think a Christian ought to look like. Many believers have bought into the idea that this is all there is to becoming more like Christ or experiencing genuine life change. Biblically, that is not what God has in mind. He promised to make you a different person, not just make you appear as a different person on the outside.

The first thing you have to understand and believe if you are going to experience authentic life change, and be a more complete image bearer of God in this world, is that all genuine, authentic life change begins with God. Not you. He is the change agent. Not you. And that goes against mankind's self-centered, independent, controlling human nature.

2. Write out Philippians 1:6 below.

3. Based on this verse, who is the initiator, sustainer and completer of life change in your life? Why is this significant?

4. Can you think of times when you have tried to make yourself a better Christian and then gave up, frustrated? What is one specific example?

5. Write out Matthew 11:28-30 below.

All authentic life change begins with God. Not you. Are you willing right now to bow the knees of your heart and cast your hard work, weariness and burdens before Him? To confess that you have made a mess of things and you are sorry for trying to do it on your own? To ask if He would take your life and make something beautiful out of the mess so others could see Him more clearly?

Turn your heart and your eyes to Him. Give Him your mess and He will give you so much more in return.

6. Write out your thoughts, feelings and desires about this to God.

Life change begins with the two most important factors in your spiritual life: your heart and your mind. They come together to form the Core of the spiritual formation process. Since all authentic life change begins with God, the Core is the first place to look for God at work in your life. This is always the primary focus of His life change process.

When your heart and mind are not both becoming more like Jesus, pride will always lift itself up and try to take control by getting you to focus on one at the expense of the other, or eventually stop focusing on either.

A Humbly Submitted heart and a Biblically Formed mind are a dynamic combination. They fuel the spiritual life and provide a tremendously fertile soil for life change to occur. As the Core generates the life of God within you, it quite naturally works its way out and begins to transform who you are on the inside and then who you are on the outside. Over time, genuine change will become evident in your life.

7. How is your heart? Is it increasingly Humbly Submitted to Jesus as the one in charge of your life? If not, who or what is the master of your heart?

8. How is your mind? Is it increasingly being Biblically Formed, or is your mind being shaped by other things? If so, what are some of those things?

God is also at work to change the kinds of choices you make in life. Your choices include your will, your desires and eventually your character: who you are becoming on the inside, reflected in the choices you make.

You make choices every day about how you will spend your time, talent and treasure (Sacrificially Generous), how you make moral and ethical decisions (Morally Discerning), how you are going to relate to others, and whether or not you are going to do the hard work of maintaining relationships (Relationally Healthy).

Scripture makes it clear that your choices come out of what is in your heart and mind. God's life change design is that He will keep developing the engine of your heart and mind, which will begin to change the way you make choices, and your choices will increasingly reflect Jesus' choices.

9. Are you a person whose choices are Sacrificially Generous, Morally Discerning and Relationally Healthy? What words best describe the kinds of motivations for the choices you are making in life?

Your compassions reveal how you see and engage the world. As the rings radiate from the center out, the elements become more and more visible to the world around you. The outermost ring of compassions (Intentional Blessing, Culturally Engaged, Inclusive Community) is the one where you are most likely to be noticed by those outside the church, and where you have the biggest opportunity to show the world more of what Jesus is like. Or not.

Because it is the most visible, the outer ring is where you are most likely to fake it, and the world will peer through your faking it and see your hypocrisy. If you don't fake it, you will either withdraw to the shelter of your own little bubble, avoiding the world, or reach out to the world around you with the love and compassion of Jesus.

God's life change design is that the engine of your heart and mind will keep developing to change the way you make choices, and your choices will increasingly spill over into your compassions and how you relate to the world.

10. Are you a person whose compassions are mostly characterized as being an Intentional Blessing, Culturally Engaged and practicing Inclusive Community? What words best describe the kinds of motivations for the compassions you are expressing in life?

11. Based on your study this week, write out your thoughts, feelings and desires to God.

WEEK 4

GOD IS AT WORK TO CHANGE YOUR HEART TO BE MORE LIKE JESUS

RECOMMENDED READING
THE ANATOMY OF A DISCIPLE CHAPTERS 5

Your heart is not just an organ that pumps blood through your body, nor is it merely the stuff of romance novels. When Jesus and biblical authors referred to the heart, they were talking about the center or essence of your life. The heart is the wellspring out of which everything else flows. It is the deep root out of which the rest of your life grows.

Phrases like, "the heart of the issue" or "the heart of the matter" are the ideas of the biblical text, that which is of first importance, out of which everything else develops.

God wants your heart to be like Jesus' heart. As your heart goes, so goes the rest of your life.

1. Write out Matthew 11:29 below.

2. How did Jesus describe His own heart?

The words *gentle* and *humble* are very similar words in the original text, though there is a slight variation of meaning. *Gentle* is the idea of not trying to force your personal desires on others, while the word for *humble* is one that depicts someone who is under authority, as opposed to the one who has to be in charge. This person appropriately puts himself or herself under the authority of another and does not resist this. Jesus described His heart as being one that did not force His ideas or wishes on others, and He saw Himself as one being under a higher authority.

3. Write out Philippians 2:5-8 below.

4. How did Paul describe the heart of Jesus in these verses?

God is changing your heart to be more like Jesus.

Being Humbly Submitted in your heart is a supernatural proposition. It is unnatural to humbly submit to anyone. Your heart, the center of your being, is naturally only submitted to you, your pleasures, your concerns. But that is the heart of stone God wants to soften and change within you to be more like Jesus' heart. And your heart will change when you dwell on Him more than on yourself.

5. Write out below what Jesus said to those who would be His disciples in Mark 8:34.

6. According to Jesus' words, what is the first thing that has to happen if you are to become His disciple? Why is this important?

7. Write out James 4:6-10 below.

8. According to these verses, how does God feel about pride in your life? What does He want your heart to be like instead?

9. Write out Matthew 5:3-6 below.

The "poor in spirit" (verse 3) are those who are bankrupt in their own spirit, devoid of any resources, as the word *poor* means here. They have tried everything, but finally come to the end of themselves as the ones who can make life happen. They are bankrupt in their own spirit and spiritual abilities, and they know it.

"Those who mourn" (verse 4) have come to realize and admit how deeply embedded sin is in their lives—to the point that it grieves them—and they mourn (as in the James passage above). Jesus said part of the maturing process is realizing and grieving over how deeply sin is embedded in your life.

"The gentle" (verse 5) do not insist on having their own way. They may have tried resisting, but have come to realize the futility of that. They give up trying to force life and others to fit into their own prescribed way of doing things, and stop trying to control their own life and others around them.

All of these words in Matthew 5:3-6 are pictures of someone progressively coming to the end of self. They have been defeated when trying to make life work on their terms and they have come to their end, which leads to the fourth statement Jesus makes.

"Blessed are those who hunger and thirst for righteousness, for they shall be satisfied" (verse 6). The words here for *hunger* and *thirst* are not describing what it is like to be hungry and thirsty because it's almost mealtime. They are terms of desperation, of feeling like you could die if you do not have something to eat and something to drink—now! This person longs to have God's kind of life: righteousness. They tried it their way and gave up on doing it on their own. If they do not have God and His kind of life right now, they cannot make it. They are desperate for Him and the life only He can provide.

This life changing progression is profound. You will never be desperate for God and His kind of life until you have come to the end of thinking and living as if you can make life work yourself. But when you do come to the end of trying to make life work on your own, deny yourself and turn to Him in desperation, He will satisfy your most desperate needs. It all begins at the center, your heart.

10. Jesus talks about our hearts in the first three beatitudes in Matthew 5:3-5. Later in the chapter He forces you to look at your own heart and see how deeply embedded sin is in your life. Write out the following verses.

Matthew 5:21-22

Matthew 5:27-28

Matthew 5:43-44

11. Jesus summarizes how good you need to be if you are going to be good enough to please God in your own efforts. Write out Matthew 5:48 below.

12. Where is your heart right now? Are you stubbornly trying to make life work on your own, or have you given up and come to God in desperation to do within you what you have not been able to do? Describe where you are right now in this process.

13. Where and how have you seen God developing your heart to be more Humbly Submitted to Him? (This may include His means of using difficult situations in your life.)

14. Based on your study this week, write out your thoughts, feelings and desires to God.

WEEK 5

GOD IS AT WORK TO CHANGE YOUR MIND TO BE MORE LIKE JESUS

RECOMMENDED READING
THE ANATOMY OF A DISCIPLE CHAPTERS 6

If the heart is your essence, the root of your motivations and actions, the mind is the lens through which you see yourself and all of life. It is not just a physical brain, but the seat of thinking, reasoning and believing. It is the perspective by which you evaluate and make choices in life.

The world is full of half-truths and good sounding lies. How these influence your heart and your actions depend on your mind. Your heart will judge your mind. Your mind will inform your heart. Your heart and mind work together and change each other over time. As your heart and mind change, so your choices and compassions will change as well.

God wants your mind to be more like Jesus' mind. But what was His mind like?

One insight into what Jesus focused on and what changed His growing mind happened right before His ministry began. He was led into the wilderness to be tempted by Satan for more than a month. Satan had successfully tempted the first man, Adam, and at that point, he set his sights on the only man without sin, Jesus Christ. As Satan tempted Jesus with the pleasantries of life without suffering, the flippant exercising of His deity, and the promise of the inheritance of all the kingdoms of this world if He would only bow down and worship Satan, Jesus' response to every temptation was the same.

1. Write out Jesus' responses to Satan's temptations below and notice what they have in common.

Matthew 4:4

Matthew 4:7

Matthew 4:10

It was the Scriptures that shaped Jesus' way of thinking, understanding and ultimately His decision-making. "It is written" was where His mind went first.

2. Where does your mind go first when challenged about what you believe or doing something you're not sure about?

3. What resources do you have for your mind go to when you need to make a decision?

Jesus' mind was saturated with the Scriptures, the truth revealed by God. It was this that motivated and led Jesus to do everything He did.

Jesus had a mind that was shaped and molded by the Scriptures. God wants your mind to be more like Jesus' mind, Biblically Formed, trained to think and see the world around you through His eyes, from a biblical point of view. He wants your thoughts and perspectives to be so shaped by Scripture that they overflow into the choices you make, and He is changing your mind to be more like Jesus.

4. Write out Romans 12:2 below.

5. What did Paul say about the mind and the impact it has on your life?

6. Write out 2 Timothy 3:16-17 below.

7. How are the Scriptures, when taken into the mind, designed to impact your life? (There are several ways mentioned in the previous passages.)

8. Paul spoke to people who refused to get in step with how God was working to change their minds to be more like His. Write out Philippians 3:18-19 below.

9. Based on these verses, what did Paul say happens to you when your mind is not focused on Scripture?

Jesus had a mind that was shaped and molded by the Scriptures. God wants your mind to be more like Jesus' mind, Biblically Formed, trained to think and see the world around you through His eyes, from a biblical point of view. He wants your thoughts and perspectives to be so shaped by Scripture that they overflow into the choices you make.

Jesus lived a life in beautiful balance with both battleground areas. His heart was Humbly Submitted to the Father and His mind was Biblically Formed. As we have seen before, these two areas working together serve as the engine of authentic spiritual life change. But when your heart and mind are out of whack, that leads to destructive behavior.

10. Write out Paul's warning in Ephesians 4:17-19 below.

11. What do you notice about the people's minds in these verses?

12. What do you notice about their hearts in these verses?

13. What did their wayward hearts and minds lead to in their behavior?

14. Do you ever feel like your behavior is out of whack? Gone wild? Disjointed? Explain.

15. Where and how have you seen God developing your mind to be more Biblically Formed?

16. As God prompts you in this area, what are the things that make it hard for you to get in step with Him and His work to fashion your mind to be more like Jesus?

17. Based on your study this week, write out your thoughts, feelings and desires to God.

WEEK 6
GOD IS AT WORK TO CHANGE YOUR GENEROSITY TO BE MORE LIKE JESUS

RECOMMENDED READING
THE ANATOMY OF A DISCIPLE CHAPTERS 7 AND 10

Within rings 3 and 4 there are sectors. The sectors demonstrate not only the direction in which life change begins to occur from the inside out, but also show the close, natural life change relationships between the elements in rings 3 and then 4.

There are three primary sectors impacted by this inside-out transformation in your life: Generosity, Morality and Relationships.

The Generosity Sector shows the natural progressive relationship between your growth in being Sacrificially Generous (Ring 3) and your growth in being an Intentional Blessing to the world

43

around you (Ring 4).

Your choices and compassions are responders to your heart and mind. You want or choose what you do because of the condition of your heart and mind. You are motivated to take a certain action or not because of the condition of your heart and mind.

As God renovates your heart and mind to be more like Jesus', your choices and compassions will begin to follow and you will start to want the things Jesus wanted and have compassion for the things Jesus had compassion for. As you live out your faith, it will inevitably overflow. Your heart, mind and choices will increasingly and directly influence the world as your compassions increasingly overflow into the world around you.

This week we will focus on how God is changing your choices to be more Sacrificially Generous and your compassions to be more of an Intentional Blessing. Over time, one naturally leads to the other.

1. Write out Matthew 4:23-24 below.

2. According to these verses, in what ways was Jesus generous with His time and talent for the benefit of others?

3. Write out below what Jesus said about Himself in Mark 10:45.

His sacrificial generosity with His own life was and is the heart of the gospel. It made Him incredibly attractive to the people around Him. Never before had they seen someone whose life was so profoundly selfless and generous with all He was and all He had. His sacrificial generosity drew a crowd and caused many to ask questions and consider their own lives. He brought light into the darkness, and through His willingness to give of Himself so freely, changed the world forever.

It is easy to see in the life of Jesus how His Sacrificially Generous choices flowed over into His compassions of intentionally blessing others, and how that impacted the world around Him.

4. Write out Mark 6:34 and 6:39-42 below.

5. How do you notice Jesus' sacrificial generosity overflow into Him being an Intentional Blessing with this crowd?

Apart from a supernatural work of God, mankind is never purely sacrificial or generous. Human nature is anything but. You might do things that seem generous or sacrificial on the outside, but down deep you do them for selfish reasons. You may give out of fear or to alleviate your guilt, or give because it makes you feel good. Your selfish pride wants to keep everything you have for yourself, and you are likely to never go out of your way for someone else unless it benefits you in some way.

God is working to change that in you. As your heart is increasingly Humbly Submitted to Him as the Master of your life, and your mind is being Biblically Formed by the truths of His Word, you will see your choices become more and more like His and your compassions more and more like His. You will increasingly become more Sacrificially Generous and an Intentional Blessing, just as Jesus was.

6. Write out 2 Corinthians 8:1-5 below.

7. What do you learn from these verses about the generosity of the Macedonians and where it came from?

8. Write out Colossians 4:12 below.

9. In what way was Epaphras Sacrificially Generous? Who do you know that is a lot like him? Describe why they remind you of Epaphras.

10. Write out 1 Peter 4:10 below.

God bestowed supernatural gifts on every believer. But no one person has all the gifts and no one gift has been given to all believers. By the very design of the body of Christ, His church, He made people to be interdependent on each other. Not independent. You need the gifts of others and they need yours.

Just as Jesus' Sacrificially Generous choices overflowed into Him being an Intentional Blessing to those who were sick, demon possessed and hungry, so God has designed you to be an Intentional Blessing to those around you.

11. Write out 1 Peter 3:8-9 below.

12. Write out Romans 12:14 below.

13. What is one opportunity to be an Intentional Blessing that you have either taken or passed up in the last week?

14. Where and how have you seen God developing your desires and involvement in being more Sacrificially Generous and an Intentional Blessing?

15. Based on your study this week, write out your thoughts, feelings and desires to God.

WEEK 7

GOD IS AT WORK TO CHANGE YOUR MORALITY TO BE MORE LIKE JESUS

RECOMMENDED READING
THE ANATOMY OF A DISCIPLE CHAPTERS 8 AND 11

Your Morality Sector includes two areas of life change: Morally Discerning and Culturally Engaged. Being Morally Discerning leads to being Culturally Engaged over time, and it also helps makes it healthier.

Because Jesus had a heart that was Humbly Submitted to His Father and a mind that was Biblically Formed, He was very discerning in areas of morality and justice. He knew the difference between right and wrong and was able to make Morally Discerning choices in the gray areas. He was acutely aware when He saw injustices, and the superficial, phony things around Him were obvious.

In one situation, the religious leaders in Jerusalem sent some spies to meet with Jesus and trick Him. Knowing the tensions in the city because of Rome's rule over the Jewish state of Israel, they asked Him if Jewish people should pay taxes to Rome.

1. Write out below what Jesus replied to them in Mark 12:15-17.

2. How were they trying to trick Jesus in these verses? How was He Morally Discerning?

3. Jesus' moral discernment was also apparent when a ruler of the Jews approached Him. Write out their dialogue below from Luke 18:18-23.

4. How would you describe the rich young ruler in this story? What about Jesus?

God designed life to work a certain way, and outside of that it gets muddled. Rights and wrongs help you know how He designed life to work for you, so you can live a full and blessed life, experiencing all the fulfillment this life has to offer. When you choose to step outside His design, your life gets blurry and increasingly messy.

5. Write out Hebrews 5:12-14 below.

The Bible says God is good. Everything God created is good in its original design. So what is evil?

Evil is not necessarily the opposite of good. Evil is any variation or distortion of what is good. God did not want mankind to constantly have to choose between that which was like God or His design and that which was different, even by the slightest degree.

6. Share a time when you thought you were doing something good, but later on realized you had done that "good" thing with selfish or wrong motives.

7. Share a time when you were in a situation where you either had or wished you had been more Morally Discerning.

Jesus' choice to be Morally Discerning impacted His compassion to be Culturally Engaged. One of the ways Jesus' compassions expressed themselves was when He stepped into other people's lives, into their cultures, and engaged them where they were. He did not wait for people to come to Him. He went to them.

Jesus used His moral discernment when deciding who to spend time with and what to do or not do as He Culturally Engaged with others who were quite different from Him. When Jesus happened to be in Samaria, a region considered unclean by the strictest Jewish people, He came upon a woman who was alone. Custom said He should never talk with her, but notice how Jesus used moral discernment in the face of custom and tradition to engage this woman in her culture.

8. Write out John 4:4-9 below.

There is a clear sense that Jesus was deeply and profoundly moved by what He saw around Him, and He entered into causes that were important to Him. He did not live a casual spectator life assuming someone else would take care of the ills of His day. Out of compassion, He engaged His culture and took issue with those He encountered. People's callousness for the poor, the mistreatment of widows and an inherent racism that was evident around Him all became issues of cultural engagement for Him. Though there were many issues Jesus chose not to get involved with, there were others that brought out His passion and His compassion, and moved Him to action.

9. One such issue that Jesus stepped into had to do with religious leaders turning God's laws around to the detriment of people instead of for their good. Write out Luke 13:15-17 below.

Being Culturally Engaged means stepping out into the world by going outside your normal sphere of comfort and opportunity, and stepping into the cultures of others, where they live, work, play and have needs. Remember, being Culturally Engaged flows from being Morally Discerning. It is in the moments where your moral discernment is energized by that growing compassion of cultural engagement that things get really exciting.

10. Write out James 2:15-17 below.

11. When was the last time you had the opportunity to engage someone who was different from you? What was your response?

12. Name two people who live in close proximity to you and one interesting thing about each of them.

    1.

    2.

13. What is one cause or issue that God has put on your heart to engage in or with? Have you engaged? If so, how? If not, what's keeping you from getting in step with what God is doing in your heart and mind?

14. Where and how have you seen God developing your desire and involvement in being more Morally Discerning and Culturally Engaged?

15. Based on your study this week, write out your thoughts, feelings and desires to God.

GOD IS AT WORK TO CHANGE YOUR RELATIONSHIPS TO BE MORE LIKE JESUS

RECOMMENDED READING
THE ANATOMY OF A DISCIPLE CHAPTERS 9 AND 12

Your Relationship Sector includes two areas of life change: Relationally Healthy and Inclusive Community. Being Relationally Healthy leads to practicing Inclusive Community over time and makes it healthier.

Jesus had healthy relationships with all kinds of people: men, women, children, friends, tax gatherers and sinners. The Gospels record how Jesus had close, healthy relationships with 12 men for over three years, until His death.

1. When it came to His family, Jesus was Relationally Healthy and knew how to set healthy boundaries with His parents. On a trip to Jerusalem from the north country of Galilee, Jesus, as a young man, stopped in the Temple to talk with the leaders. While having a very lively discussion with them, His parents came in. Write out Luke 2:48-49 below.

2. What do you notice in this interaction between Jesus and His mother? How did she speak to Him? How did He respond?

3. Later Jesus showed one final act of relational health regarding His relationship with His mother Mary as He was dying on the cross. Write out John 19:26-27 below.

4. What do you learn about Jesus and the importance of relationships to Him in these verses?

5. One of the marks of Christian maturity is found in the nature and health of your relationships—at all levels, in all your relationships. Jesus even summed up the teachings and desires of God. Write out Matthew 22:37-40 below.

6. On a scale of 1-10, with 1 being very unhealthy and 10 being exceptionally healthy, how would you rate your marriage relationship (if married)? Why?

7. On a scale of 1-10, how would you rate your family relationships? Why?

8. On a scale of 1-10, how would you rate your friend relationships? Why?

9. On a scale of 1-10, how would you rate your work or school relationships? Why?

10. On a scale of 1-10, how would you rate your willingness to resolve conflicts? Why?

11. God designed you to live in relationships and be healthy in them, and He wants to change the things that lead to hard relationships. So what does the Bible say about how to heal hurt or broken relationships? One clear picture is from Paul's letter to the church in Colossae. Write out Colossians 3:12-16 below.

12. What can you glean about healthy relationships from these verses?

Notice that Paul told them part of the key to their relationships was their hearts and minds (verses 15-16). If you are relationship-challenged, don't forget that the place to start is the Core, your heart and mind.

13. Jesus had deep and meaningful, healthy relationships with a number of people. Notice how being a Relationally Healthy person made it possible for Him to reach out to others who were not in His circle of already established friends and include them in His life. Write out Luke 5:27-32 below.

14. What do you learn from Levi in this story? What about Jesus?

You were brought to Christ and left here on this earth to be a light that shows Him off, a leader who steps into the world as His hands and feet, and a lover who invites others into your life to meet Him more personally. Jesus Christ did not die on the cross to simply secure heaven for you someday, but rather to develop you into a living illustration of God to those around you today.

15. Why is it so challenging to be a living demonstration of God for the world to see?

16. Write out 2 Corinthians 5:14-15 below.

17. What insight does this passage provide about why it is challenging to be a living demonstration of God to others?

God is working in your life to make you someone of His love, because He is love, and His kind of love is in both word and deed. It is empty to say God loves people and yet not ever let them see God's love in your actions. You will seldom see people respond to God's message of love in the gospel until they see the gospel of love have an impact on their everyday lives. Jesus' life was a masterful blend of both words and deeds of love and compassion.

18. Where and how have you seen God developing your desire and involvement in being Relationally Healthy and practicing Inclusive Community?

19. Based on your study this week, write out your thoughts, feelings and desires to God.

WEEK 9
GOD IS WORKING TO HELP YOU GET BACK IN STEP AND STAY IN STEP WITH HIM

RECOMMENDED READING
THE ANATOMY OF A DISCIPLE CHAPTERS 15 AND 17

So far throughout this study you have seen the natural or ideal flow of maturity God designed for you, yet there are many factors that come into play that challenge that ideal. Everyone is wired differently, and everyone has different personalities and bents. And of course we all mess up, because all humans are fallen creatures due to the sin factor.

1. You are going to get knocked down, and you will mess up. That is not news to God. He is not surprised. God has accounted for all that. Notice how Paul described God's involvement in your life, even when you wrestle with sin and choose to live life outside His designed order. Write out Romans 8:26-28 below.

2. What are some of the ways this passage shows that God is working to help you in your weakness and propensity to mess up?

3. Another way God works to help you get back on track is found in the following passage. Write out Hebrews 12:11 below.

4. Sometimes God will lavish His love on you in the midst of your pain to remind you how precious you are to Him and to lift you up from the mire—to even help others when they are facing the same kind of pain. The Apostle Paul saw this in his own suffering. Write out 2 Corinthians 1:3-5 below.

Have you ever found yourself in a painful situation or wrestling with sin or a failure and your first prayer is, "God, take this away" or "Take this sin away from me. I'm sick of it" or "Take this hurt away from me. I can't take it anymore" or "Take these consequences away from me. I don't want to face them anymore"? Have you ever stopped to consider that maybe God is using some of those hard things in your life to help you grow?

What if the dynamic Christian life was not some kind of joy ride, but was about your maturity? You may be there as part of the maturing process that God is allowing you to go through so you can become more like Him.

5. Can you recall a prayer you've said for God to take something away from your life, but later you realized maybe God was allowing that in your life to help you grow or help you get back in step with Him? Explain.

6. Write out James 1:2-4 below.

7. How does this passage align with what you have been learning this week?

It is a very different thing for you to take responsibility to make yourself change to be like Jesus than to understand that He is the one changing you, and then get in step with what He is doing already. God is going to be about changing you, whether you know it or not. Even if you do not like what He is doing in you. Even if you do not like the method He is choosing to change you. The question is, "Are you going to get in step with Him and His plan for your life change, or resist and try to do it on your own, in your own way?"

Regardless of your answer, He is in charge and is changing you. Both ways will likely involve pain in one form or another, to one degree or another. But getting in step with Him and what He is doing will be much more productive and effect greater life change than you could ever make happen on your own. Doing it your own way will be increasingly frustrating and self-defeating. You will experience a downward cycle of frustration and failure until—until the sheer agony of it will draw you back to your knees, where you needed to be anyway. Back to the Core.

8. In his letter to the Ephesian Christians, the Apostle Paul reminded them of the world they had been a part of and stepped out of. He painted a picture of how, in the past, their hearts and minds had been distorted and disfigured from God's design, and how that had led them to make very ungodly choices in their lives, causing them to become callous and not at all compassionate. Write out below his words from Ephesians 4:17-19.

9. Are you weary from trying hard, only to fail and mess up again? Write out Matthew 11:28-30 below.

The Bible calls Christians to *obey*. The root of the word obey means to "hear" or "listen," and do so with an attitude of willingness to respond properly. God is at work. Are you listening? Are you aware of what He is doing? Do you have an attitude of willingness to get in step with what God is doing?

As God moves in your life, He reveals things in you that you need to be aware of. It may be God is revealing an area of pride or a spiritual blind spot. It may be recognizing common temptations or patterns of sin. It may be as intense as uncovering deep pain in your past that shapes your present or as simple as revealing something from the Word that He wants you to respond to. Regardless of what God is showing you, there needs to be awareness of what He is doing in your life. Half the battle spiritually is remembering that it begins and ends with Him and then developing an awareness of what He is actually showing you.

10. Write out Galatians 5:16 below.

11. Paul goes on in the above passage to explain what God will produce as you walk in step with what God is doing in your life instead of trying to change yourself. Write out Galatians 5:22-23 below.

12. Where has God been at work in your life? How have you responded to this work He is doing?

13. Based on your study this week, write out your thoughts, feelings and desires to God.

WEEK 10
MAKING
THIS
YOURS

This week is for helping you make The Anatomy of a Disciple your own as well as equip you to help others understand how God helps each of us grow.

1. Ask 2-3 Christians you know to describe where they are at spiritually. Write a summary of their responses below.

    1.

    2.

    3.

2. Ask these same Christians if they have ever had someone explain to them what a mature Christian looks like and how God designed for us to grow to become like that ideal, and if so, what is that process like? Write a summary of their responses below.

1.

2.

3.

3. Write out Philippians 1:6 below.

4. What is the significance of this verse in explaining God's plan for life change?

5. In the blank Anatomy of a Disciple graphic below, fill in the eight characteristics of a disciple who is becoming more like Jesus. (Be sure to keep the sectors together.)

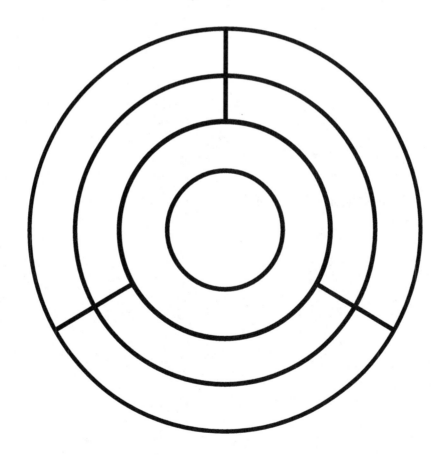

6. God is changing your heart to be

_____ _____.

What does this mean?

7. God is changing your mind to be

_____ _____.

What does this mean?

8. What is the significance of the Core in God's life change process?

9. God is changing your choices to be

_____ _____.

What does this mean?

10. God is changing your choices to be

_____ _____.

What does this mean?

11. God is changing your choices to be

_____ _____.

What does this mean?

12. God is changing your compassions to be an

_____ _____.

What does this mean?

13. God is changing your compassions to be

_____ _____.

What does this mean?

14. God is changing your compassions to practice

_____ _____.

What does this mean?

15. What is the most significant change you have seen in your Core? Explain.

16. What is the most significant change you have seen in your choices? Explain.

17. What is the most significant change you have seen in your compassions? Explain.

18. Write down the names of 1-3 people you think might be interested in going through this discipleship process with you.

   1.

   2.

   3.

19. Write a prayer of thanks to God for what He has done and is doing in your life to make you more like Jesus. (Some of these things may be exciting and some may be hard. Think about these things.)

CPSIA information can be obtained
at www.ICGtesting.com
Printed in the USA
FSOW04n2051150716
22819FS